Thoughts of Thoreau

RICHARD CAMERON

ISBN: 1502547775
ISBN-13: 978-1502547774

DISCLAIMER

While every effort has been made to ensure the information in this book is correct, human error is always a possibility and therefore the author cannot accept responsibility for any inaccuracies.

CONTENTS

INTRODUCTION

Henry David Thoreau (1817 – 1861), born in Concord, Massachusetts, was one of America's most original thinkers and forward-looking philosophers. He was an early abolitionist against the slave trade, a teacher and believer in practical education in which real experiences, such as nature walks and visits to businesses were valued more than just words in a classroom. He was a skilled poet, essayist and a champion of the environment, an early ecologist.

Today he is rightly admired; but in his day his influence was slight. He was dismissed as an anarchist for advocating less governmental control over people's lives. Yet as an advocate of passive resistance and civil disobedience, he influenced such later figures as Tolstoy, Gandhi and Martin Luther King.

He preferred a simple life that was in tune with nature

and much of his writing foreshadows our own age of concern for the environment.

Although not as widely known as many other American writers, Thoreau's wisdom is well worth our attention. In this book you will find a collection of his wisdom and beliefs told in short quotations from his works.

ABOUT HIMSELF

"I have a great deal of company in the house,
especially in the morning when nobody calls."

*

"I love to be alone. I never found the companion that
was so companionable as solitude."

*

"I did not wish to take a cabin passage, but rather to
go before the mast and on the deck of the world, for
there I could best see the moonlight amid the
mountains. I do not wish to go below now."

*

"I have always been regretting that I was not as wise as the day I was born."

*

"I would rather sit on a pumpkin and have it all to myself, than be crowded on a velvet cushion."

*

"When I hear music, I fear no danger. I am invulnerable. I see no foe. I am related to the earliest times, and to the latest."

*

"There are old heads in the world who cannot help me by their example or advice to live worthily and satisfactorily to myself; but I believe that it is in my power to elevate myself this very hour above the common level of my life."

*

"I have been as sincere a worshipper of Aurora as the Greeks."

*

"In my afternoon walk I would fain forget all my morning occupations and my obligations to society."

*

"I had three chairs in my house; one for solitude, two for friendship, three for society."

*

"If I knew for a certainty that a man was coming to my house with the conscious design of doing me good, I should run for my life."

*

"I was more independent than any farmer in Concord, for I was not anchored to a house or farm, but could follow the bent of my genius, which is a very crooked one, every moment."

*

"I put a piece of paper under my pillow, and when I could not sleep I wrote in the dark."

*

"The greatest compliment that was ever paid me was when one asked me what I thought, and attended to my answer."

FRIENDS

"Nothing makes the earth seem so spacious as to have friends at a distance; they make the latitudes and longitudes."

*

"The most I can do for my friend is simply be his friend."

*

"Friends... they cherish one another's hopes. They are kind to one another's dreams."

*

"True friendship can afford true knowledge. It does not depend on darkness and ignorance."

*

"The language of friendship is not words but meanings."

*

"There is danger that we lose sight of what our friend is absolutely, while considering what she is to us alone."

GENERAL PHILOSOPHY

"To affect the quality of the day, that is the highest of arts."

*

"All this worldly wisdom was once the unamiable heresy of some wise man."

*

"There is no rule more invariable than that we are paid for our suspicions by finding what we suspect."

*

"Disobedience is the true foundation of liberty. The obedient must be slaves."

*

"I think that there is nothing, not even crime, more opposed to poetry, to philosophy, ay, to life itself than this incessant business."

*

"Night is certainly more novel and less profane than day."

*

"Do what nobody else can do for you. Omit to do anything else."

*

"As in geology, so in social institutions, we may discover the causes of all past changes in the present invariable order of society."

*

"If misery loves company, misery has company enough."

*

"It is the greatest of all advantages to enjoy no advantage at all."

*

"It is a characteristic of wisdom not to do desperate things."

*

"The fibers of all things have their tension and are strained like the strings of an instrument."

*

"That government is best which governs least."

*

"I say beware of all enterprises that require new clothes, and not rather a new wearer of clothes."

*

"Any fool can make a rule, and any fool will mind it."

*

"Our inventions are wont to be pretty toys, which distract our attention from serious things. They are but improved means to an unimproved end."

*

"They can do without architecture who have no olives nor wines in the cellar."

*

"Our houses are such unwieldy property that we are

often imprisoned rather than housed by them."

*

"We shall see but a little way if we require to understand what we see."

*

"I have found that hollow, which even I had relied on for solid."

*

"None are so old as those who have outlived enthusiasm."

*

"The language of excitement is at best picturesque merely. You must be calm before you can utter oracles."

*

"To a philosopher all news, as it is called, is gossip, and they who edit and read it are old women over their tea."

*

"There is one consolation in being sick; and that is the possibility that you may recover to a better state than you were ever in before."

*

"Under a government which imprisons any unjustly, the true place for a just man is also a prison."

*

"'Tis healthy to be sick sometimes."

*

"There is no just and serene criticism as yet."

HAPPINESS

"Wealth is the ability to fully experience life."

*

"What is called genius is the abundance of life and health."

*

"That man is rich whose pleasures are the cheapest."

*

"There is no value in life except what you choose to place upon it and no happiness in any place except what you bring to it yourself."

*

"A man is rich in proportion to the number of things he can afford to let alone."

*

"Make the most of your regrets; never smother your sorrow, but tend and cherish it till it comes to have a separate and integral interest. To regret deeply is to live afresh."

HUMANKIND

"I have thought there was some advantage even in death, by which we mingle with the herd of common men."

*

"The man who is dissatisfied with himself, what can he do?"

*

"If a man does not keep pace with his companions, perhaps it is because he hears a different drummer. Let him step to the music which he hears, however measured or far away."

*

"Every man casts a shadow; not his body only, but his imperfectly mingled spirit. This is his grief. Let him turn which way he will, it falls opposite to the sun; short at noon, long at eve. Did you never see it?"

*

"Those whom we can love, we can hate; to others we are indifferent."

*

"All men are children, and of one family. The same tale sends them all to bed, and wakes them in the morning."

*

"Every people have gods to suit their circumstances."

*

"Every generation laughs at the old fashions, but follows religiously the new."

*

"Why should we be in such desperate haste to succeed, and in such desperate enterprises? If a man does not keep pace with his companions, perhaps it is because he hears a different drummer."

*

"It is an interesting question how far men would retain their relative rank if they were divested of their clothes."

*

"If I seem to boast more than is becoming, my excuse is that I brag for humanity rather than for myself."

*

"In human intercourse the tragedy begins, not when there is misunderstanding about words, but when

19

silence is not understood."

*

"We are always paid for our suspicion by finding what
we suspect."

*

"Is the babe young? When I behold it, it seems more
venerable than the oldest man."

*

"It is not part of a true culture to tame tigers, any
more than it is to make sheep ferocious."

*

"I have found that no exertion of the legs can bring
two minds much nearer to one another."

*

"There never was and is not likely soon to be a nation of philosophers, nor am I certain it is desirable that there should be."

*

"Men have become the tools of their tools."

*

"It is usually the imagination that is wounded first, rather than the heart; it being much more sensitive."

*

"Generally speaking, a howling wilderness does not howl: it is the imagination of the traveler that does the howling."

*

"The mass of men lead lives of quiet desperation. What is called resignation is confirmed desperation."

*

"Thank God men cannot fly, and lay waste the sky as well as the earth."

*

"The savage in man is never quite eradicated."

*

"The youth gets together his materials to build a bridge to the moon, or, perchance, a palace or temple on the earth, and, at length, the middle-aged man concludes to build a woodshed with them."

*

"Dreams are the touchstones of our character."

*

"The heart is forever inexperienced."

*

"I have never found a companion that was so companionable as solitude. We are for the most part more lonely when we go abroad among men than when we stay in our chambers. A man thinking or working is always alone, let him be where he will."

*

"Things do not change; we change."

KNOWLEDGE

"Nay, be a Columbus to whole new continents and worlds within you, opening new channels, not of trade, but of thought."

*

"I have seen how the foundations of the world are laid, and I have not the least doubt that it will stand a good while."

*

"Our moments of inspiration are not lost though we have no particular poem to show for them; for those experiences have left an indelible impression, and we are ever and anon reminded of them."

*

"Where there is an observatory and a telescope, we expect that any eyes will see new worlds at once."

*

"It is only when we forget all our learning that we begin to know."

*

"Books can only reveal us to ourselves, and as often as they do us this service we lay them aside."

*

"Being is the great explainer."

*

"Not until we are lost do we begin to understand

ourselves."

*

"How many things there are concerning which we might well deliberate whether we had better know them."

*

"This world is but a canvas to our imagination."

*

"As a single footstep will not make a path on the earth, so a single thought will not make a pathway in the mind. To make a deep physical path, we walk again and again. To make a deep mental path, we must think over and over the kind of thoughts we wish to dominate our lives."

*

"A truly good book teaches me better than to read it. I must soon lay it down, and commence living on its hint. What I began by reading, I must finish by acting."

*

"The universe is wider than our views of it."

*

"Books are to be distinguished by the grandeur of their topics even more than by the manner in which they are treated."

*

"It is too late to be studying Hebrew; it is more important to understand even the slang of today."

*

"Books are the treasured wealth of the world and the fit inheritance of generations and nations."

*

"Men have a respect for scholarship and learning greatly out of proportion to the use they commonly serve."

LIFE

"It is what a man thinks of himself that really
determines his fate."

*

"Through our own recovered innocence we discern
the innocence of our neighbors."

*

"Live your life, do your work, then take your hat."

*

"The cost of a thing is the amount of what I will call
life which is required to be exchanged for it,
immediately or in the long run."

*

"Many men go fishing all of their lives without
knowing that it is not fish they are after."

*

"How vain it is to sit down to write when you have
not stood up to live."

*

"Our life is frittered away by detail... simplify,
simplify."

*

"As you simplify your life, the laws of the universe
will be simpler; solitude will not be solitude, poverty
will not be poverty, nor weakness weakness."

*

"I went to the woods because I wished to live deliberately, to front only the essential facts of life, and see if I could not learn what it had to teach, and not, when I came to die, discover that I had not lived."

*

"There is no more fatal blunderer than he who consumes the greater part of his life getting his living."

*

"Every creature is better alive than dead, men and moose and pine trees, and he who understands it aright will rather preserve its life than destroy it."

*

"Nature and human life are as various as our several constitutions. Who shall say what prospect life offers to another?"

*

"How could youths better learn to live than by at once trying the experiment of living?"

*

"The price of anything is the amount of life you exchange for it."

*

"So thoroughly and sincerely are we compelled to live, reverencing our life, and denying the possibility of change. This is the only way, we say; but there are as many ways as there can be drawn radii from one centre. All change is a miracle to contemplate; but it is a miracle which is taking place every instant."

*

"Our truest life is when we are in dreams awake."

*

"Some are reputed sick and some are not. It often happens that the sicker man is the nurse to the sounder."

*

"Do not trouble yourself much to get new things, whether clothes or friends... Sell your clothes and keep your thoughts."

*

"Live the life you've dreamed."

LOVE

"Do what you love. Know your own bone; gnaw at it,
bury it, unearth it, and gnaw it still."

*

"Ignorance and bungling with love are better than
wisdom and skill without."

*

"There is more of good nature than of good sense at
the bottom of most marriages."

*

"May we so love as never to have occasion to repent
of our love!"

*

"There is no remedy for love but to love more."

*

"Do not hire a man who does your work for money,
but him who does it for love of it."

MONEY

"Money is not required to buy one necessity of the soul."

*

"To have done anything just for money is to have been truly idle."

RICHARD CAMERON

.

MORALITY

"After the first blush of sin comes its indifference."

*

"Not only must we be good, but we must also be
good for something."

*

"It is best to avoid the beginnings of evil."

*

"The perception of beauty is a moral test."

*

"Instead of noblemen, let us have noble villages of men."

*

"Aim above morality. Be not simply good, be good for something."

*

"While civilization has been improving our houses, it has not equally improved the men who are to inhabit them. It has created palaces, but it was not so easy to create noblemen and kings."

*

"The law will never make a man free; it is men who have got to make the law free."

*

"In the meanest are all the materials of manhood, only they are not rightly disposed."

*

"If the machine of government is of such a nature that it requires you to be the agent of injustice to another, then, I say, break the law."

*

"The squirrel that you kill in jest, dies in earnest."

*

"It is not desirable to cultivate a respect for the law, so much as for the right."

*

"Do not be too moral. You may cheat yourself out of much life so. Aim above morality. Be not simply good; be good for something."

*

"Goodness is the only investment that never fails."

*

"It is never too late to give up our prejudices."

*

"Be not simply good - be good for something."

*

"There are a thousand hacking at the branches of evil to one who is striking at the root."

*

"What is human warfare but just this; an effort to make the laws of God and nature take sides with one party."

*

"How does it become a man to behave towards the American government today? I answer, that he cannot without disgrace be associated with it."

*

"Justice is sweet and musical; but injustice is harsh and discordant."

*

"There is no odor so bad as that which arises from goodness tainted."

*

"An unclean person is universally a slothful one."

*

"If you would convince a man that he does wrong, do right. Men will believe what they see."

RICHARD CAMERON

NATURE

"What is the use of a house if you haven't got a tolerable planet to put it on?"

*

"Nature is full of genius, full of the divinity; so that not a snowflake escapes its fashioning hand."

*

"Nature puts no question and answers none which we mortals ask. She has long ago taken her resolution."

*

"There are moments when all anxiety and stated toil are becalmed in the infinite leisure and repose of nature."

*

"To be admitted to Nature's hearth costs nothing. None is excluded, but excludes himself. You have only to push aside the curtain."

*

"An early-morning walk is a blessing for the whole day."

*

"It is remarkable how closely the history of the apple tree is connected with that of man."

*

"A man's interest in a single bluebird is worth more than a complete but dry list of the fauna and flora of a town."

*

"The bluebird carries the sky on his back."

*

"There are certain pursuits which, if not wholly poetic and true, do at least suggest a nobler and finer relation to nature than we know. The keeping of bees, for instance."

*

"Shall I not have intelligence with the earth? Am I not partly leaves and vegetable mould myself?"

*

"Nature will bear the closest inspection. She invites us to lay our eye level with her smallest leaf, and take an insect view of its plain."

*

"Thaw with her gentle persuasion is more powerful than Thor with his hammer. The one melts, the other breaks into pieces."

"In wildness is the preservation of the world."

*

"Alas! how little does the memory of these human inhabitants enhance the beauty of the landscape!"

*

"It appears to be a law that you cannot have a deep sympathy with both man and nature."

*

"If a man walks in the woods for love of them half of each day, he is in danger of being regarded as a loafer. But if he spends his days as a speculator, shearing off those woods and making the earth bald before her time, he is deemed an industrious and enterprising citizen."

SPIRITUALITY

"Most of the luxuries and many of the so-called comforts of life are not only not indispensable, but positive hindrances to the elevation of mankind."

*

"What lies behind us and what lies ahead of us are tiny matters compared to what lives within us."

*

"God reigns when we take a liberal view, when a liberal view is presented to us."

*

"Faith keeps many doubts in her pay. If I could not doubt, I should not believe."

*

"If it is surely the means to the highest end we know, can any work be humble or disgusting? Will it not rather be elevating as a ladder, the means by which we are translated?"

*

"Heaven is under our feet as well as over our heads."

*

"The smallest seed of faith is better than the largest fruit of happiness."

*

"We must learn to reawaken and keep ourselves awake, not by mechanical aid, but by an infinite expectation of the dawn."

*

"Faith never makes a confession."

*

"Pursue some path, however narrow and crooked, in which you can walk with love and reverence."

SUCCESS

"Live your beliefs and you can turn the world around."

*

"We must walk consciously only part way toward our goal, and then leap in the dark to our success."

*

"If you have built castles in the air, your work need not be lost; that is where they should be. Now put the foundations under them."

*

"A man cannot be said to succeed in this life who does not satisfy one friend."

*

"Great men, unknown to their generation, have their fame among the great who have preceded them, and all true worldly fame subsides from their high estimate beyond the stars."

*

"What is once well done is done forever."

*

"The Artist is he who detects and applies the law from observation of the works of Genius, whether of man or Nature. The Artisan is he who merely applies the rules which others have detected."

*

"Success usually comes to those who are too busy to be looking for it."

*

"We are not what we are, nor do we treat or esteem each other for such, but for what we are capable of being."

*

"Only he is successful in his business who makes that pursuit which affords him the highest pleasure sustain him."

*

"If you can speak what you will never hear, if you can write what you will never read, you have done rare things."

*

"The finest workers in stone are not copper or steel tools, but the gentle touches of air and water working at their leisure with a liberal allowance of time."

*

"It is not enough to be busy. So are the ants. The question is: What are we busy about?"

*

"What you get by achieving your goals is not as important as what you become by achieving your goals."

*

"What old people say you cannot do, you try and find that you can. Old deeds for old people, and new deeds for new."

*

"I know of no more encouraging fact than the unquestionable ability of man to elevate his life by conscious endeavor."

*

"I learned this, at least, by my experiment: that if one advances confidently in the direction of his dreams, and endeavors to live the life which he has imagined, he will meet with a success unexpected in common hours."

*

"Men are born to succeed, not to fail."

*

"If we will be quiet and ready enough, we shall find compensation in every disappointment."

*

"In the long run, men hit only what they aim at. Therefore, they had better aim at something high."

*

"Nothing goes by luck in composition. It allows of no tricks. The best you can write will be the best you are."

THE PRESENT MOMENT

"The light which puts out our eyes is darkness to us. Only that day dawns to which we are awake. There is more day to dawn. The sun is but a morning star."

*

"Never look back unless you are planning to go that way."

*

"It is better to have your head in the clouds, and know where you are... than to breathe the clearer atmosphere below them, and think that you are in paradise."

*

"You must live in the present, launch yourself on every wave, find your eternity in each moment."

TIME

"Time is but the stream I go a-fishing in."

*

"Read the best books first, or you may not have a
chance to read them at all."

*

"A broad margin of leisure is as beautiful in a man's
life as in a book. Haste makes waste, no less in life
than in housekeeping. Keep the time, observe the
hours of the universe, not of the cars."

*

"The man who goes alone can start today; but he who travels with another must wait till that other is ready."

*

"As if you could kill time without injuring eternity."

*

"Before printing was discovered, a century was equal to a thousand years."

TRUTH

"Could a greater miracle take place than for us to look through each other's eyes for an instant?"

*

"Rather than love, than money, than fame, give me truth."

*

"No face which we can give to a matter will stead us so well at last as the truth. This alone wears well."

*

"Truth is always in harmony with herself, and is not concerned chiefly to reveal the justice that may consist with wrong-doing."

∗

"The rarest quality in an epitaph is truth."

∗

"Truths and roses have thorns about them."

∗

"The lawyer's truth is not Truth, but consistency or a consistent expediency."

∗

"It's not what you look at that matters, it's what you see."

∗

"I am sorry to think that you do not get a man's most effective criticism until you provoke him. Severe truth is expressed with some bitterness."

*

"It takes two to speak the truth: one to speak, and another to hear."

ALSO BY RICHARD CAMERON

UKIP'S PARTY POOPERS